F HORN

HOLIDAY FAVORITES

Solos and Band Arrangements
Correlated with Essential Elements® Band Method

Arranged by ROBERT LONGFIELD, JOHNNIE V...
MICHAEL SWEENEY and PAUL LAVENDE...

T0081645

Welcome to Essential Elements Holiday Favorites! There are two versions of each selection in this versatile book. The SOLO version appears in the beginning of each student book. The FULL BAND arrangement of each song follows. The ONLINE RECORDINGS or PIANO ACCOMPANIMENT BOOK may be used as an accompaniment for solo performance. Use these recordings when playing solos for friends and family.

PLAYBACK+
Speed • Pitch • Balance • Loop

To access audio visit:
www.halleonard.com/mylibrary

Enter Code
7586-2343-6846-7155

ISBN 978-1-5400-2796-2

HAL•LEONARD®

Visit Hal Leonard Online at
www.halleonard.com

00870014

Contact Us:
Hal Leonard
7777 West Bluemound Road
Milwaukee, WI 53213
Email: info@halleonard.com

In Europe contact:
Hal Leonard Europe Limited
42 Wigmore Street
Marylebone, London, W1U 2RN
Email: info@halleonardeurope.com

In Australia contact:
Hal Leonard Australia Pty. Ltd.
4 Lentara Court
Cheltenham, Victoria, 3192 Australia
Email: info@halleonard.com.au

AULD LANG SYNE

Words by ROBERT BURNS
Traditional Scottish Melody
Arranged by MICHAEL SWEENEY

F HORN
Solo

FELIZ NAVIDAD

F HORN
Solo

Music and Lyrics by
JOSÉ FELICIANO
Arranged by PAUL LAVENDER

3

PARADE OF THE WOODEN SOLDIERS

F HORN
Solo

English Lyrics by BALLARD MacDONALD
Music by LEON JESSEL
Arranged by PAUL LAVENDER

00870014

GOOD KING WENCESLAS

F HORN
Solo

Words by JOHN M. NEALE
Music from PIAE CANTIONES
Arranged by ROBERT LONGFIELD

00870014

PAT-A-PAN
(Willie, Take Your Little Drum)

F HORN
Solo

Words and Music by
BERNARD de la MONNOYE
Arranged by ROBERT LONGFIELD

SILVER BELLS

F HORN
Solo

Words and Music by
JAY LIVINGSTON and RAY EVANS
Arranged by PAUL LAVENDER

00870014

DO YOU HEAR WHAT I HEAR

F HORN
Solo

Words and Music by
NOEL REGNEY and GLORIA SHAYNE
Arranged by MICHAEL SWEENEY

From THE SOUND OF MUSIC

MY FAVORITE THINGS

F HORN
Solo

Lyrics by OSCAR HAMMERSTEIN II
Music by RICHARD RODGERS
Arranged by ROBERT LONGFIELD

00870014

From the Motion Picture Irving Berlin's HOLIDAY INN

WHITE CHRISTMAS

F HORN
Solo

Words and Music by
IRVING BERLIN
Arranged by JOHNNIE VINSON

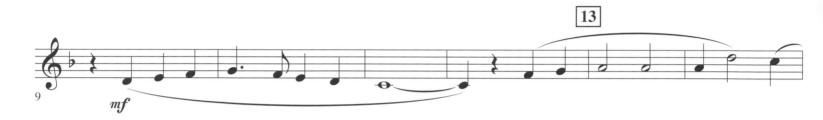

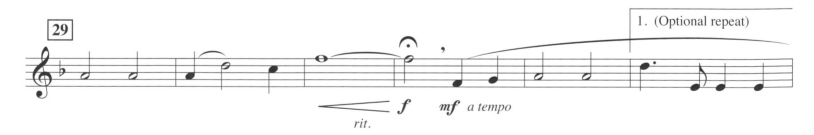

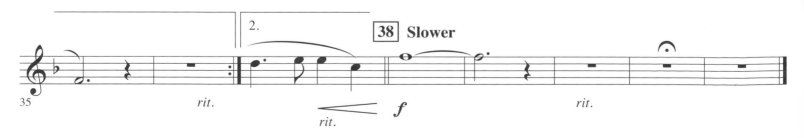

CHRISTMAS TIME IS HERE

F HORN
Solo

Words by LEE MENDELSON
Music by VINCE GUARALDI
Arranged by JOHNNIE VINSON

From Warner Bros. Pictures' THE POLAR EXPRESS

THE POLAR EXPRESS

F HORN
Solo

Words and Music by
GLEN BALLARD and **ALAN SILVESTRI**
Arranged by JOHNNIE VINSON

AULD LANG SYNE

F Horn
Band Arrangement

Words by ROBERT BURNS
Traditional Scottish Melody
Arranged by MICHAEL SWEENEY

FELIZ NAVIDAD

F HORN
Band Arrangement

Music and Lyrics by
JOSÉ FELICIANO
Arranged by PAUL LAVENDER

PARADE OF THE WOODEN SOLDIERS

F HORN
Band Arrangement

English Lyrics by BALLARD MacDONALD
Music by LEON JESSEL
Arranged by PAUL LAVENDER

00870014

GOOD KING WENCESLAS

F HORN
Band Arrangement

Words by JOHN M. NEALE
Music from PIAE CANTIONES
Arranged by ROBERT LONGFIELD

PAT-A-PAN
(Willie, Take Your Little Drum)

F HORN
Band Arrangement

Words and Music by
BERNARD de la MONNOYE
Arranged by ROBERT LONGFIELD

00870014

Silver Bells

F HORN
Band Arrangement

Words and Music by
JAY LIVINGSTON and RAY EVANS
Arranged by PAUL LAVENDER

DO YOU HEAR WHAT I HEAR

F Horn
Band Arrangement

Words and Music by
NOEL REGNEY and GLORIA SHAYNE
Arranged by MICHAEL SWEENEY

00870014

From THE SOUND OF MUSIC

MY FAVORITE THINGS

F HORN
Band Arrangement

Lyrics by OSCAR HAMMERSTEIN II
Music by RICHARD RODGERS
Arranged by ROBERT LONGFIELD

From the Motion Picture Irving Berlin's HOLIDAY INN

WHITE CHRISTMAS

F HORN
Band Arrangement

**Words and Music by
IRVING BERLIN**
Arranged by JOHNNIE VINSON

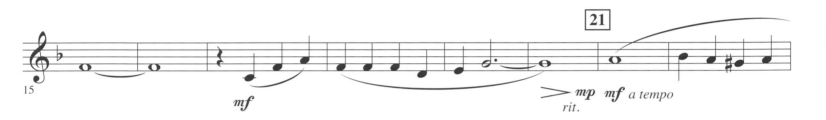

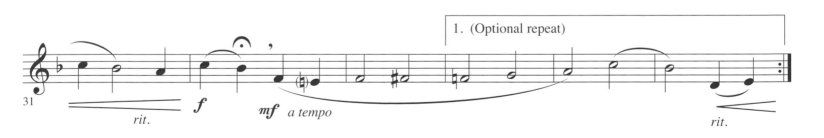

00870014

CHRISTMAS TIME IS HERE

F HORN
Band Arrangement

Words by LEE MENDELSON
Music by VINCE GUARALDI
Arranged by JOHNNIE VINSON

Moderately Slow, Smoothly

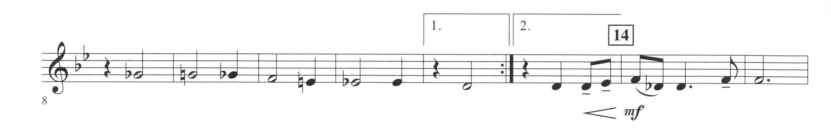

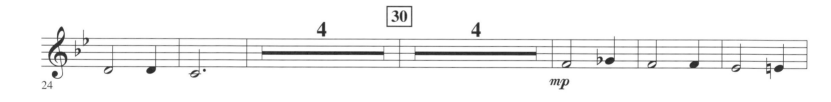

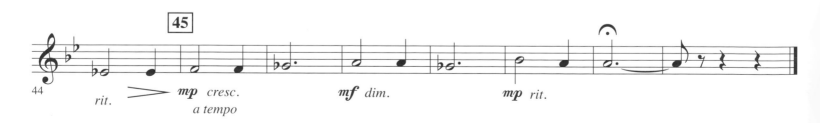

From Warner Bros. Pictures' THE POLAR EXPRESS

THE POLAR EXPRESS

F HORN
Band Arrangement

Words and Music by
GLEN BALLARD and **ALAN SILVESTRI**
Arranged by JOHNNIE VINSON